the growth principle
how ordinary people do extraordinary things

G.J. Barnes

May you continue to soar in every area you tackle

Outskirts Press, Inc
Denver, Colorado

The opinions expressed in this manuscript are solely the opinions of the author and do not represent the opinions or thoughts of the publisher. The author represents and warrants that he either owns or has the legal right to publish all material in this book.

The Growth Principle
How Ordinary People Do Extraordinary Things
All Rights Reserved.
Copyright © 2008 G.J. Barnes
V4.0 R1.1

This book may not be reproduced, transmitted, or stored in whole or in part by any means, including graphic, electronic, or mechanical without the express written consent of the publisher except in the case of brief quotations embodied in critical articles and reviews.

Outskirts Press, Inc.
http://www.outskirtspress.com

ISBN: 978-1-4327-2644-7

Outskirts Press and the "OP" logo are trademarks belonging to Outskirts Press, Inc.

PRINTED IN THE UNITED STATES OF AMERICA

The Growth Principle

G.J. Barnes

The book is dedicated to the lady who taught me to dream big: my mother Ralene B. Barnes

The Growth Principle

I would like to acknowledge my family, church family, friends, neighbors and colleagues for the encouragement and inspiration to discover growth. I especially would like to thank my wife Junetta, for her priceless contribution of long hours, encouragement, and creativity.

The Growth Principle

The Table of Contents

Chapter 1: The Growth Principle 7

Chapter 2: Identify Your Vision 17

Chapter 3: Going Beyond You 29

Chapter 4: Committed to the Vision 37

Chapter 5: Explore Your Seeds 47

Chapter 6: Evaluate Your Environment 55

Chapter 7: Nurture Your Seeds 63

Chapter 8: Work Your Plan 73

Chapter 9: Things That Hinder Your Work 79

Chapter 10: Have Faith in Your Success 89

Chapter 11: Strengthen Others 95

Appendix 100

Chapter 1: The Growth Principle

Remember that the person who plants few seeds will have a small crop; the one who plants many seeds will have a large crop.
(2 Corinthians 9:6 GNB)

Over the years, I have often wondered, just exactly how did people accomplish great things. I would learn about people who made great historical contributions, gained prominent reputations and built lucrative businesses, and be fascinated. This fascination led me to a litany of questions ranging from why did they become accomplished, to what really drove their success? I wondered was achievement something that happened by chance or did people use a system to fulfill their dreams and see their visions come to fruition.

Originally, I always assumed that extraordinary accomplishments, strides and monumental achievements came *from* people who were privileged in some way. I was sure they came from a well-connected family, and had unprecedented resources. But, as I studied people's lives, and read people's biographies, I soon discovered a more genuine truth regarding the journey of extraordinary accomplishers. I learned that a great majority of people, who accomplished extraordinary things, were actually *ordinary* in many respects. There were many who experienced major difficulties, numerous setbacks, and had a nice cadre of folk who didn't believe in their future. The truth was that many extraordinary accomplishers weren't necessarily child-geniuses, or well-connected with powerful people. This revelation made me even more curious about the experiences of these ordinary people and the way they went on to achieve exceptional things. This curiosity and interest led me to take a more systematic look at the journey of those who were achievers. The result of that inquisition is the ideas that are expressed in this book, which can all be summed up in *The Growth Principle*.

The Growth Principle in some form or another has been used in every single case of significant achievement. This principle continues to be a foundation for uplifting everyday people to conquer remarkable obstacles. People have maximized their potential, and empowered others all because somewhere along the line, they were introduced to the essence of *The Growth Principle*.

The Growth Principle

Although powerful and significant, *The Growth Principle* is still quite simple. Its substance goes back to the beginning of time, but is still as potent today as ever before. What's the foundation of *The Growth Principle*? The answer is simply to remember a seed that's planted and nurtured will grow and produce fruit. *The Growth Principle* is a principle based on sowing and reaping. It's based on investments and returns. *The Growth Principle* is about planting seeds, nurturing seeds, and experiencing the fruit.

The kind of seeds we're talking about isn't grass seeds, or flower seeds, or even an apple tree seed. So the kind of fruit we're talking about here isn't apples or oranges. But, the type of seeds we're focused on are seeds that are shaped in the form of an idea, vision, goal, thought, plan, strategy, or anything of the like. Moreover, the type of fruit we're talking about here is continued *extraordinary accomplishment*. In other words, the seed is what will be planted inside your heart & mind, and when nurtured with the principles that are presented in this book, will grow bountifully and produce the fruit of extraordinary accomplishment.

This growth that we talk about is significant because it is purposeful and powerful. Why, because it has changed lives. So *The Growth Principle* is simply about planting ideas, nurturing ideas, and producing the fruit of extraordinary accomplishment. This principle of planting and nurturing becomes essential to personal growth, just as it's essential to the growth of a plant. Unfortunately, too many of us desire growth, but never implement the principle of planting our ideas or desires and cultivating those ideas or desires. This book is about learning how to plant, nurture and reap the fruit of our seeds.

Growth Principle Characteristics

As I looked and studied people who displayed this principle, I saw some similarities among their choices and characteristics. The first thing I noticed was that they all kept a unique idea in their minds, no matter the circumstances they faced. That unique but simple idea was to never give up. These extraordinary accomplishers sometimes had to face rejection (which you will see later in this book), failure, or even ridicule, but they kept perseverance central to their way of thinking. Even though we may have heard the word perseverance many times before, it's essential to manifesting *The Growth Principle* and maximizing our potential.

Never giving up is the first thing you must understand in your journey of achieving growth. The bottom line is that, no matter where you are in life or what

The Growth Principle

accomplishments you may have attained, you must never give up on growth, because there is always room for growth and extraordinary achievement. It doesn't matter if you are a college student, an advisor to the President of the United States, or a single parent with a ninth grade education, there is always room to increase your potential and grow toward your remarkable accomplishment.

The second major similarity among people who displayed impressive achievement was a passion to learn. People who see the world as a source of knowledge capture information and inspiration that propel them toward outstanding results. Once a seed is planted, learning is a major way it is nurtured. Extraordinary accomplishers are always reading books, and always traveling to new places. They discover the importance of learning & absorbing the many traditions, discoveries and ideologies that give them perspective. Although many of us may not possess the time or have the financial means to travel the world, we do have the ability to adapt a mindset of curiosity and discovery.

"Attitude is more important than Intelligence."
- Dr. David Schwartz

The third similarity among achievers was their attitude and approach to the world. To make your seed flourish and exercise *The Growth Principle*, you must have a *Moving Forward Mentality*, or what we'll call for short a "**Moform**." There are many times when people will desire growth and significant accomplishment, but will not be willing to let go of some things from the past. Sometimes these past ideas can hinder us from moving forward to pursue growth and change. But, if we don't expect to move forward and increase our potential, how will we ever accomplish growth? The definition of Moform is simply making a decision that you will move forward and embark on the journey of change. It's when you may have to say to yourself "enough is enough" or "I'm confident in my future success." This is when we determine in our minds that going backward isn't an option and that moving forward is the only attitude we'll embrace.

The one thing I have learned in life is to never rest on the accomplishments or failures of the past, because our potential grows everyday. In other words, our potential isn't based by our past, but connected to our determination in the present.

The fourth similarity of extraordinary accomplishers was in their level of motivation, although not just any type of motivation. Considerable accomplishers acquire genuine motivation about growth. They are known as

The Growth Principle

being intrinsically motivated regarding their achievements and ideas.

Intrinsic motivation is when a person is motivated by his or her pure desire to participate in something for its own sake and no other reason. For instance, if a person takes a job where they have to talk a lot, solely because they love talking to people, they are intrinsically motivated to work. However, if a person takes a job where they have to talk a lot, solely because they want to make more money, and hate talking to people, they are not intrinsically motivated, but extrinsically motivated to work.

Extrinsic motivation is defined as a person being motivated by rewards, gifts, or anything that is an outside incentive. Another example is if a child gets an A on a math exam because they love math, they study with an intrinsic motivational drive. However, if a child that gets an A on their math exam because their father promised him $10 for an A, then they probably studied with an extrinsic motivational drive.

It is good to point out that extrinsic motivation isn't all bad per se. It surely does work when trying to get your kids to clean their rooms, or your toddler to stay in his seat. But as you can see, extrinsic motivation is really only good if you have a fancy treat waiting at the other end. That's why being motivated to do something without getting any outside incentive is what will last in the long run. Imagine if you want to lose weight only because of an upcoming hot date. But in an unfortunate turn of events, the hot date you dreamed of cancels early. Then guess what, your motivation for losing weight is also cancelled early.

That's why if you want your journey of growth to last and to see an abundance of fruit, you must be sure you're not doing it for some outside "treat." Instead, be sure you're doing it because you believe in growth and are dedicated to increasing your potential. Many extraordinary accomplishers never seek to be on the cover of a popular magazine, or get a movie made about their journey. These accomplishers instead seek personal growth, knowledge and the satisfaction of achievement.

The Growth Principle

Reflections

1. What am I currently doing to increase my knowledge-base?

_____
_____
_____
_____
_____
_____

2. What things in life am I intrinsically motivated about?

_____
_____
_____
_____
_____
_____

3. What challenges have I given up on?

_____
_____
_____
_____
_____
_____

Chapter 2: Identify Your Vision

Where there is no vision, the people perish.
Proverbs 29:18

Just imagine if you were driving on a remote highway, not familiar with your surroundings, and with every passing minute becoming more lost. You finally see a small pit-stop restaurant on the side of the road, and you're sure that somebody there can help you with your journey. You go in and see a man who looks like a veteran truck driver and proceed to ask him for directions.

The first thing the truck driver asks you is "where are you going?" You say to him, "I don't quite know where I'm going, but I'm sure that I want to get there." I'm completely sure you guessed what would happen next. The truck driver with all of his navigational knowledge and highway experience will not be able to help you on your journey. I always tell people that "without a destination, you can have no direction." So the first step in extraordinary achievement and applying the growth principle is identifying your seed and having a vision for the future and sticking to that pledge.

    The second thing we must realize is that our seed or vision must go beyond ourselves. For instance, if the seed that we're trying to plant is only to get more money, so we can brag, act ostentatious and not help others when we are able to do so, then our seed's potential is sadly limited. It's okay to want to be financially free, but that shouldn't come at the expense of your character or by becoming pretentious and not lending a hand to your neighbor through outreach and charity. We've got to realize that all of our blessings aren't simply to go *to us*. They have more power and effectiveness when they go *through us*. Isn't it interesting that when you survey history, many of the world's richest people gave away the most money? Sure you may be saying that they gave away the most money because they had the most, and proportionately that would make sense.

    But I always have to remind myself that they *didn't* have to give. Logically, if they didn't give, they could have had even more money, but with their large giving, not only were they able to keep their standard of living, they left a legacy that continues to give to others even to this day. Think of people like Andrew Carnegie, Anthony J. Drexel,

The Growth Principle

Johns Hopkins, Alfred Nobel, John D. Rockefeller, or Cornelius Vanderbilt. These individuals didn't allow their seeds to stop with them, but as you know, their seeds are still producing fruit even to this day. The point that I'm suggesting here is that your seed or vision must always go beyond yourself, and a selfish seed never leaves a legacy.

Third when understanding your seed, make sure you don't focus too much on the problems that can prevent your growth. Your focus should predominately be on your destination and fulfillment of your vision. Often times, when people are confronted with the idea of growing or achieving extraordinary accomplishments, they are overtaken by the "what about this" litany. It can frequently begin with the "what about my limitations" or the "what about the obstacles," questions. And those questions can be relevant at times, but the key isn't that you don't ask those questions, but the key is that you don't focus on those questions. The focus should be on solutions and destinations, and not problems and obstacles. Solutions will say "yes, we can" and problems will try to tell you "no, we can't."

Any small business owner will tell you that in the business world, there is never a shortage of problems. Either your employees just quit on you, and it's hard to find replacements, or your supplier raised her costs by 20 percent, and you just can't raise your prices. There is always a problem that begs a solution. However, as a business owner, I continually tell myself that it is my duty to focus on my pledge of determination and not just the problems of the day.

There are days when the problems pile-on like players diving for a fumbled ball in an overtime super bowl game, and there's plenty of hopelessness to go around. However, I have to continually tell my wife and staff that too much focus on the problem can influence us to forget about our pledge.

I've learned that focusing too much on the problem can lure us into a mode where we actually begin to follow our problems. This type of focus often leads to reactive decision-making, instead of following our pledge and making proactive decisions that propel our moform. When people make reactive decisions, they make decisions based on reacting simply to problems; their direction soon begins to follow the path of problems, as opposed to the path of our destination. Without fail, *proactive decisions are always more sustaining than reactive ones.*

A reactive decision-making routine will have people performing maintenance and not moving with mission. Just think if I have 10 problems that posed a threat to my current position, and focus just on those ten problems throughout my day, even if I solve them, I have not made

The Growth Principle

any net gain. I'm just in the position of where I was before I had those 10 problems.

Even outside of developing our vision, it's important to not let problems distract us from our pledge. We should develop a daily boundary system that limits how much time and energy we give to problems & negative issues, to ensure our net gain of achievement. Although it is important to recognize and attend to problems, we must be sure that we deal with them within our set limits.

Mark Ashcroft, a psychologist who conducted research at the University of Nevada Los Vegas, studied what he called math anxiety. He, along with others, did research that showed when people focused on math as a "problem," they created what's called math anxiety. This math anxiety then preoccupies their minds so much that it contributes to actually doing worse in math. Dr. Ashcroft said that when people focus so much on math itself being a problem "… math anxiety occupies a person's working memory." Therefore, *the act of focusing or worrying about a problem can actually make the problem worse.*

This is why I made a pledge to myself that dealing with daily problems will never get more than about 10 percent of my focus for that day. Therefore, problems will not become the forefront of my thoughts or that day's preoccupation. At the same time, I make sure that ideas, actions and meetings related to growth and creating vision take at least 30 percent of my day. This is what I call the 30% rule. In that way, I make sure that growth is the foremost thing that occupies my mind. Sure there are issues and maintenance decisions that one must attend to, but the 30% rule ensures that everyday I'm spending a fair amount of my time on things that keep me moving forward. So, as we create our vision, and even outside of creating our vision, it is important to stay focused on our pledge of accomplishment and not on our litany of problems.

The fourth thing we must do when creating the vision for our future is to simply write it down and make it easy to read. The Bible says that God told the prophet Habakkuk that He had a message for him through a vision and he was to: "write the vision and make it plain..."

The point here is that once you get an understanding of your vision for the future, you must be able to articulate it and write it down. Research has shown for years that writing down something can increase the chances that it will be etched in your memory and therefore implemented. This is why many people take notes in classrooms and write reminders on small pads. The act of writing increases the chance that something will be memorized.

Writing down your vision for the future not only increases your chances of remembering it, but also helps

The Growth Principle

clarify your vision to yourself and others. Many people have ideas and thoughts about what their futures should look like, but often only with a vague and general description. The truth is that *clarity will influence effectiveness*. So, when people clarify their visions ideas and thoughts, they can expect to be more effective in the long run in implementing their visions and seeing fruit. In addition, it is wise to have no more than three different items when writing down your vision at any one time. It's good to control your focus to about three things at a time, so you don't get so overwhelmed with tons of objectives and goals that you get none of them done.

Furthermore, writing down your vision does more than just help you remember it, and clarify your thoughts; it also helps you stay accountable. With your vision written down, there is now another level of accountability that rests with your pledge of achievement. No longer is it just something you said vaguely months ago; now, it's something that is clear and written down, and you can refer back to it when your motivation level begins to drop. It also allows you to have an accountability partner. After you've written down your vision with clarity and purpose, you can copy that vision and give it to an accountability partner who can encourage and remind you about your journey to extraordinary achievement (see the appendix for my family's foundational statement).

When reflecting on my college days, sometimes I can remember doing pretty well in my classes, and sometimes I can remember struggling to get a B. Yet, if I took a class with a friend, and we held each other accountable for knowing the material and getting an A, we gave each other momentum to reach our goal. When we surround ourselves with the right people to encourage us and hold us accountable, we increase the likelihood of manifesting our vision and seeing its fruit.

The truth of vision and its impact on later events in life can be seen many times throughout history. There were people who never gave up, made sure their fruit went beyond them and even wrote down their seeds to plant. I was inspired after reading the life story of Wilma Rudolph and how her vision of her future enabled her to overcome all of the past difficulties, obstacles, and limitations that were placed on her by other people. She had a vision that was workable and challenging, and didn't give up until the seeds she planted grew.

Wilma Rudolph

Wilma was born to a big family, the 20th of 22 children, and was born prematurely. From the beginning of her life, people didn't expect her to accomplish much, let

The Growth Principle

alone even live to adulthood. However, she survived her birth. At the age of 4, she had another obstacle to overcome. She became very sick as a result of a serious illness and was left paralyzed in her left leg. By the age of 13, she managed to walk again through determination and God's miraculous favor. That same year, she began to develop a vision for her future. Though it was challenging and she was laughed at, she developed a vision to be a runner.

People couldn't understand why she was chasing after something that wasn't possible, but she knew in her heart it was workable. So, she entered into races and marathons. Over the next few years, she came in last place at every race. Nevertheless, she believed that her present wasn't something that would limit her future. She kept on fighting and believing and planting seeds of victory that one day, due to her hard work, she would actually win a race. In fact, she went on to win three gold medals at the 1960 Summer Olympics.

Applying the growth principle and reaching extraordinary accomplishment, all begins with vision. This vision is what you see that others don't necessarily see, and others won't necessarily believe. But, this vision is something that you believe in, and it should be something that can drive you to extraordinary achievement for years to come.

Reflections

1. What kind of legacy would I like to leave for future generations?

_____
_____
_____
_____
_____
_____
_____
_____
_____
_____

2. What type of vision would I like to fulfill in 5 years?

_____
_____
_____
_____
_____
_____
_____
_____
_____
_____
_____
_____

Chapter 3: Going Beyond You

In life, we can make the mistake of becoming comfortable in our everyday existence. We like how things are going; we enjoy our routine; and we are experts at life. Some of us even believe there is no need for change, and there is no need for growth. They live by the adage, "If it isn't broken, don't fix it." But, the truth of life is that anything that isn't growing soon dies. The reality is that even if a person doesn't experience a physical death, they can experience a mental or spiritual one.

One thing that I've learned from my studies of change is that all change isn't growth, but all growth *is* change. The fact that something is growing means that something is changing. Growing up in this life is a collection of periods that mark distinct change. From a baby to a toddler, a child must learn to explore his world and decrease his dependency on his mother. From a toddler to a small child, he must learn to change, accept responsibility for his actions and begin formal education. From a child to an adolescent, he must learn to change and use his mind for more complex thinking. You get the point: growth marks change.

People often don't change because they think it is something bad, or they are unmotivated (for the most part), but overwhelmingly people don't change because they are *afraid* of change. People are afraid of change, because it represents the unknown, and many people are afraid of things they don't know. *Fear of the unknown is the number one driver that makes people avoid the highway of change.*

Several people fear the unknown, due to the possibility they will end up worse off than they are now, failing, or even being rejected. They are not willing to take a chance or risk their humiliation. Many surveys show that the number one fear in western society is not dying, or even losing a loved one, but public speaking. This was the biggest fear people experienced, not because they were afraid of getting hit with tomatoes or of being shocked by the microphone, but because speaking to a crowd is something new that could bring humiliation or rejection.

"What if I do a terrible job?" or "what if people reject me?" or "what if my voice sounds ridiculous?" One

The Growth Principle

figures if they are humiliated in front of one person, the impact is only one person, but if they are humiliated in front of a crowd, the impact is exponential. These are some examples of thoughts that plague people's mind and hold them back from change. However, just as you can tell yourself the negative outcomes of change, you can tell yourself the positive outcomes of change. Remember the math anxiety we talked about in chapter 2? Thinking a situation will turn out badly can actually influence it for the worse. Research shows that the idea of "self-fulfilling prophesies" may have some meat to it. But, it's also important to realize that the opposite is also true: believing your situation can turn out for the better can actually make your outcome better.

As I look through the Bible, and read the Gospels, I am fascinated with the miraculous works of Jesus the Christ and His disciples. We see things, such as sickness, death, blindness, sadness or other negative things confronted by God's power, and people are instantly healed or set free. However, it is interesting to note that often the healing, or breakthrough that Jesus delivered was dependent on one thing. That one thing was the recipients' faith. Jesus often said that "according to your faith…" you would receive your desires and accomplish great things *through* Him.

Jesus helped us understand that our beliefs can influence our destiny, all the way to the point of salvation. The Bible says in Roman 10:9 that if we believe in our hearts and confess with our mouths that Jesus Christ is Lord, we will be saved. Essentially, our eternal life is not based on what we do or where we've been, but on our faith and what we believe. Jesus said in Matthew 21:22, "If you believe, you will receive whatever you ask for in prayer."

We must realize that our fears are unfounded. Sure we may fail or be rejected by others, but that doesn't stop us from reaching extraordinary accomplishments and growing to fulfill our vision of the future.

What to do about rejection?

The key I've learned concerning rejection is to be prepared for it, don't be disturbed by it. One of the biggest things that stop people from changing is fear and the experience of rejection. After some people face rejection, they find it difficult to place themselves in a vulnerable position and fear the possibility of facing rejection again. They make choices and have relationships, or lack thereof, that are designed to be rejection-resistant. This can been seen in the mother who doesn't let family members get close by not showing up for family events, or in the father who will not express authentic feelings for fear of ridicule. However, through the wisdom of many successful people, we have learned that rejection is something that should not stop change and growth.

It's important to understand that rejection isn't a projection about our future, but just a subscript of our past. In other words, rejection isn't something that has to determine your future. In order for us to let go of the fear of change, we must interpret rejection in the correct way. When we experience rejection, we know that our success is getting closer, and that it's just releasing us to a better opportunity. Realize that having a positive mindset about rejection is not just some form of denial or rationalization about the rejection we experience, but it is a genuine truth. *Be prepared for rejection, but don't be discouraged by it.*

Chester Carlson

There is a man of our time who displays the courageous action of moving forward in change in the face of rejection. His name is Chester Carlson. Chester grew up in a household where he was exposed to a life-load of work. Due to his parent's disabilities, he had to do many things at a young age to keep the household running. Growing up, he seemed to be interested in things that involved graphics and loved learning about publishing.

G.J. Barnes

In later years, he worked hard, went to college to receive a degree in physics, and then continued his education to graduate from law school and specialize in patent law. With all of his experience and passion, after 15 years of hard work, he completed his prize invention. However, to his dismay, he presented his great invention not 1, 2, or 3, but to 20 corporations, and they all gave him a firm taste of rejection. He would change his presentation, or alter his exhibit, but still all the corporations rejected his idea.

However, *even after seven straight years of rejection, he still wouldn't give up* on his invention and decided to continue and move forward with his passion. He knew that changing his invention would put him in uncharted territory, but he kept his belief in success and moved forward. In 1947, a small company named The Haloid Company purchased the rights to his invention, which was later called the electrostatic paper-copying process. The company that purchased those rights became a pivotal company in modern history. That company's new name soon become Xerox.

Just as Mr. Carlson had to face rejection and charter unknown territory, we have the ability to go beyond ourselves (our fear, hesitation, etc.) and achieve extraordinary accomplishments.

Reflections

1. How has fear stopped my progress in the past?

_____
_____
_____
_____
_____
_____
_____
_____
_____
_____

2. What things in the past have I been afraid to change and why?

_____
_____
_____
_____
_____
_____
_____
_____

Chapter 4: Committed to the Vision

Commitment breeds persistence, and persistence breeds results. Research and wisdom tells us that commitment is something that can be stronger than any amount of intelligence, any amount of money, and any size army. It has been proven over and over again that commitment can save a marriage, save a family, or even save a soul.

Knowing that we need to be committed to our vision is essential to applying *The Growth Principle* and realizing our fruit. There are many people that start off with ambitions and dreams, and are on their way to extraordinary achievement in their lives, but in the swift change of an instant, an act of failure shows up. For example, they followed their passion, which was for them to start a business, but their first month of business didn't even bring in enough money to cover the cost of their initial advertising.

These circumstances can be very frustrating and can bring discouragement to your front door faster than an express overnight delivery. I know, because I've been there all too often. But, the lesson that I, along with others, have learned is to keep the commitment to your vision and fruit in the forefront of your life, no matter what happens.

Thomas Edison
I love the often-told story of Thomas Edison and his quest to create the light bulb. His idea and passion were set, and his motivation was high, but his initial results were not so bright. However, with all the reason in the world to stop and quit, he stayed committed to his vision, no matter the results. His first 100 experiments were not fruitful; his second set of 100 experiments was incorrect, and his third set of 100 prototypes didn't work. It reportedly took him approximately 2000 failed prototypes and experiments before he manifested a completed product.

Before we embark on the journey of applying *The Growth Principle*, it is important that we are committed to our vision and to increasing our potential. Commitment is something that will fight against the swings of failure and the bullets of unbelief. Commitment can protect us from missing out on a blessing simply because we gave up. It is important to ask ourselves, what are we really committed to?

The Growth Principle

If you had to make a list of 10 things that you are committed to no matter what happens in your life, what would they be? Would they be things related to your family, things related to your faith, or things related to your life-purpose? What about things related to your friends and your professional career? Imagining what you would be committed to could bring insight and understanding to your motivations and ideas.

Staying committed to the vision: personal testimony

This story all started when God gave me the vision to further my education by attending college. Now, as I was browsing through college bulletins and college marketing publications, there were plenty of schools that were seemingly within my reach. Just about every public school in Maryland was on my list, but I came to find out through the application process, that I wasn't on their list. So, after I realized that years of goofing off in high school had finally caught up with me, I began considering technical education, or going to a community college. Even though I had worked my way up to wanting and believing in going to a four-year college, I could see the colleges' point, given my late application, my low

SAT score, and my low grades. Because of this, I would be grateful to get into a community college without all remedial courses.

So, after I didn't get into the schools I thought I was going to get into, I got a letter from a school's admission office, and the first word was "congratulations." Now, throughout this college application process, I had never seen a letter start with "congratulations," so things were starting to look up. As I read the letter, I was invited to an enrichment program that allowed motivated students who had an inferior academic high school life to redeem themselves in their first two semesters of college. Because it took me to then to figure out how important school would be in my life, I was motivated more than ever to prove myself and to fulfill the vision that God had given me. So, I enrolled in the school, which to some people would look like my only option, and began to work very diligently.

I began to prove myself as a true "academician," but I soon realized that going to a private school would cost me a lot more than just curfews at night. It would cost me a whopping $20,000+ a year. Now as I looked at the tuition cost and at my wallet, I began to pray. I said "God, I do believe this is the vision you have for my life, and I've read in the Bible, that 'My God will supply all my needs according to His riches in Christ Jesus,' and for sure your

The Growth Principle

child is in need." I was fortunate to muster up about $16,000 in loans, scholarships, and grants, but when financial clearance time came around for the next year, I couldn't enroll in school without paying my $4,100 bill in full in about 7 days.

I couldn't believe that I only had 7 days to come up with $4,100. I thought "impossible, my parents don't have that kind of money sitting around." I couldn't even gather up $400 by myself, and I didn't have any known super-rich relatives or friends. So, I began to question what in the world I was going to do. Could I sell my blood or a kidney? Could I sign a record contract? I was getting desperate.

However, in the midst of all this confusion, a sense of peace, that seemed to surpass, or outdo all of my understanding, fell over me, and I began to tell myself, "If God brought me too it, He's faithful in bringing me through it."

I figured God had brought me to college, so now the bill is on Him. After I began to change my perspective, I went to the financial office to appeal my case, and basically the college said it would give me eight days instead of seven, but if I couldn't pay the money, I was gone. I kindly told the financial officer I would surely have the money, in full, because I just believed. I also asked her to just believe with me. So, she kind of gave me that, we'll see look, like, "We've heard this before, but we need our money in eight days."

Now, just to back up a bit, this all happened in January, and as the year came in, I attended the New Year's Eve service at church, where I worked at the time as the Youth Minister of Music. In that particular service, we tend to get a lot of visitors and members, so it's almost like a packed Easter holiday service. This service, however, had a sort of local celebrity attend. He was a Baltimore Ravens football player or former player (I forget which) and he was led by God to donate $10,000 to the church on the spot. The donor decided to take key individuals from my church to dinner to celebrate the next week. Now, all this was going on at the same time I was asking God for $4,100 and hoping and believing I would get it.

Now I had mentioned to my pastor that I needed the money, but the church wasn't quite in the position to cut a check for $4,100, so my pastor was concerned and prayed for me. That day, I proceeded to purchase my school supplies and study for early tests, because I believed I would surely finish school. About two days after I had gone to the school's office, telling them I would have the money, my church went to dinner with the donor and his

The Growth Principle

business associate. At the dinner, they talked and talked about the church and its vision.

My (now late) mother had attended the dinner. As soon as she got home that night, she called me to tell me all about the details of the evening. When I got back to my dorm room that night from running various errands, I had a message on my phone from my mother instructing me to give her a call that night, as soon as I could no matter the time. So, putting down my bags and taking off my coat, I figured, before making rounds of phone calls to friends, I'd give my mother a call just to see what she wanted.

When I called my mother, she told me about the dinner they had and how the donor had paid for everybody's meal, which was well over $500, and how they had discussed some new topics. She told me about how the donor's business associate was led to also make a donation to the church, and the church was to give it to someone they saw fit who needed the money at that time. My mother also told me that as the business associate had talked with members of the church, the name of a certain person had been brought to the table as being in a financial crisis that was worthy of help.

The business associate felt that it was her calling to relieve this troubled individual from the financial strain and to bless them with their needed payment in full. By the time my mother told me who the individual in financial crisis was and how they already had a check written for them, I was jumping up and down so much I think I had to drop the phone. The individual was, of course, me, and I knew with all my heart that it was the work of God that made that possible.

    To this day I understand the concept that staying committed to your vision, no matter the circumstances, will always pay off. I was so happy to march up to that office on only day three and provide them with a check to pay my account in full. Some people may not believe in modern-day miracles, but I surely do, and the copy of the $4,100 check is on my wall as a reminder that God is still in the miracle business.

The Growth Principle

Reflections

1. How many things have I accomplished because of commitment?

_____
_____
_____
_____
_____
_____
_____
_____
_____

2. How many things *haven't* I accomplished because of commitment?

_____
_____
_____
_____
_____
_____
_____
_____
_____
_____

Chapter 5: Explore Your Seeds

A wise man will hear and increase learning, and a man of understanding will attain wise counsel.
Proverbs 1:5

The vision is clear, concise, and ready to go. We understand change is important, and we are no longer afraid of rejection. Now the time has come to think more directly about the practice of *The Growth Principle*. We must remember that any seed planted and nurtured will grow, so it's time to explore and discover which seeds to plant to grow the vision that is placed in our hearts.

Seeds can be as simple as smiles or as complex as doctoral programs, but they all should serve a purpose: to manifest the vision for our lives and lead us to the fruit of extraordinary accomplishment. The truth is that we are all familiar with seeds, because we have all been using them all of our lives. Even if we aren't in a place that we find desirable, it was an undesirable seed that contributed to where we are.

However, now it's time to think about the seed that will get us to our new destination and keep us increasing our potential. There is an endless amount of seeds to choose from, so it will benefit us to have a system in place to help us choose the most appropriate seeds. We want to make sure that a system is in place to help us choose seeds, manage seeds, cultivate seeds, and harvest the fruit.

The way we will build this system is by going to back to our vision. We see a vision and believe that we can achieve it, so we first must learn the things that are required to sustain the vision.

For example, if our vision was to be a better spouse, and we were clear in our vision that it requires us to spend more time with our spouse, then that would be the beginning seed on the list of requirements for our vision. We would then look at what is required for us to spend more time with our spouse, and we would explore and discover that, such as the need to develop time management skills.

After we discovered time management was required to be able to spend more time with our spouse, we would then look at what was required for time management to happen. We could say that in order for time management to

The Growth Principle

happen, I've got to plan my day, and, for that to happen, I need to get a calendar. Your requirements may very well be different, but this is the process that will get you to discover the requirements of your vision. You would eventually end up with a pyramid system that would show what foundational requirements have to be fulfilled first in order for other requirements to be fulfilled.

The pyramid on the next page shows visually that to get to the top of the pyramid, which is to become a better spouse, there are in this example, four steps that should lead you to your vision. Notice that you start from the bottom of the list and work your way up until you get to the top. These four steps that will lead you to the top are chronological, and are the seeds that you will plant and nurture to get to the vision of your future and increase your potential.

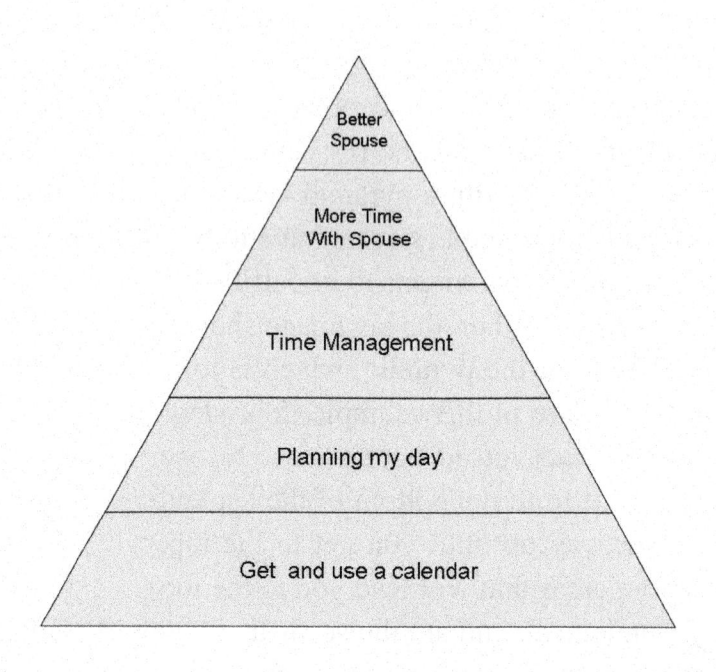

```
        Better
        Spouse
      ───────────
      More Time
      With Spouse
    ───────────────
    Time Management
  ───────────────────
    Planning my day
 ─────────────────────
  Get and use a calendar
```

In this example, you begin with a simple seed of getting and using a calendar. So you plant the action of purchasing a calendar (paper or software) and you also plant the idea of using that calendar to organize your day. After you have planted that seed, you would have to nurture it by continually putting all your appointments, events and engagements on your calendar.

Just as a seed not nurtured with water and sunlight won't grow, a seed not nurtured (in this case) with appointments and events won't grow. After this seed is

The Growth Principle

planted and nurtured, you see the next seed up is planning your day. Once you have all the events and appointments in place, you have to plant the seed of making decisions to stay on task with the plan that is written on your calendar. If there are appointments and events on a calendar and you don't follow them, then the purpose of the calendar has been lost.

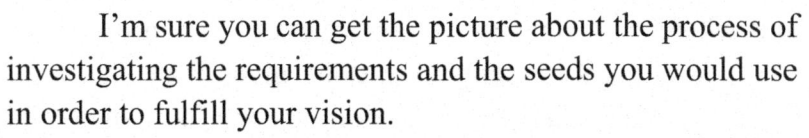

I'm sure you can get the picture about the process of investigating the requirements and the seeds you would use in order to fulfill your vision.

"Analyze Before you Act."

\- Peter F. Drucker

Now as one explores these requirements and seeds, it is important to make sure that you diversify your resources as much as possible. It is wise not to assume that you have all the answers concerning the requirements and seeds that need to be planted in order to manifest your vision. It is important to seek wise counsel and conduct sound research and exploration.

If you have a friend that has experience regarding the vision for your future, it is good to use him or her as a resource to help determine your requirements and ways to plants personal seeds. If you want to reach extraordinary accomplishment, for instance, learning another language, consult people and books who can share the requirements and seeds that have to be planted to learn that language. This system of mapping out your requirements and graphing your personal seeds will help tremendously in ensuring that your process is organized, efficient and effective.

It is important to remember that when many people think about change, they think only about where they are, and where they want to be. This process of charting your requirements not only gives you the final destination of your vision, but also the milestones involved in getting to your vision. We often forget to define what the transition stages will look like, or how it will feel to be 30 percent complete or 60 percent complete. When you have your steps on paper, you can easily track your progress. At the end of the book, there is a blank pyramid that can help you explore your seeds, to facilitate your vision and extraordinary accomplishment.

The Growth Principle

Reflections

1. What seeds are needed for me to accomplish my vision?

___

2. What resources have I used to determine my seeds?

___

Chapter 6: Evaluate Your Environment

I can remember when my wife and I were excited about moving into our new house. We had tons of ideas about how we were going to decorate the rooms. We wanted a comfortable feel in the kitchen, and a sleek feel in the office. We wanted a fun feel in the basement and an academic feel in the learning center. However, when it came to our own personal bedroom, we wanted something tropical, relaxing and unique. So we decided that palm trees, ocean paintings and flower-print patio furniture would give us the look and feel we were after.

As we were populating our room with furniture, we decided to get four palm trees to go in our room. Two would go in the sitting area (they were artificial) and the other two (they were real majestic palm trees) would go by our bed and in the bathroom. We enjoyed our trees the first few weeks after they arrived, and we were so impressed with the trees' presence. Although we were keeping up with the maintenance of our two real palm trees, we soon noticed that the leaves began to die and it seemed like nothing we were doing would prevent this loss. We pruned the leaves, kept them wet and even made sure they had sunlight, but the leaves kept dying to our disappointment.

I quickly became worried and started to seek advice. I began to reference several horticultural books and Web sites that were palm-tree specific. As I perused through the material, I came across one article that seemed to describe our symptoms to the letter. I read this article and got down to the section where the author began to describe the causes of the symptoms we were seeing. The author simply wrote that the core problem was the trees' environment. The author wrote that sometimes in homes where the air is dry and the temperature is low, it is very difficult to grow palm trees regardless of the amount of sunlight and water.

I then realized that even though I was doing so much to try to keep our trees alive, I was going through an uphill battle. We've got to understand in life that our environment will have a major impact on our growth. It can either support and cultivate our growth, or it can damage and restrict our growth. It is important that we apply the Growth Principle and reach extraordinary

The Growth Principle

accomplishment by staying in an environment that fosters growth.

Even in times when we can't change our physical environment, we still have the power to alter our mental environment. For example, if we know that certain friends produce an environment that hinders growth, it would benefit us to separate ourselves from them. If we know that certain social events hinder us from the growth we seek, we must separate ourselves from those events.

Sure, there are times when people have to endure unfortunate circumstances and difficult environments that may seem to hinder their potential. There are places where people have to be, and they don't have a choice to change their surroundings. In these circumstances, it is important to ask whether you really have to stay in that specific environment. Moreover, people can find hope and expectation through the technique of creating what I call sub-environments.

A **sub-environment** is a physical, mental or spiritual surrounding (environment) someone places themselves in when they can't physically get out of a hindering environment. This technique can work with people who may have been incarcerated, confined to a hospital, or cannot get out of a neighborhood that is detrimental to their progress. People can still increase their potential, even if they can't immediately physically change their environment, because they have the power to create a sub-environment that can foster growth and lead to extraordinary accomplishment.

How to create a sub-environment

The best way to create an effective, positive sub-environment is to follow two main steps. The first main step is to remove negative stimulation from your surroundings. Negative stimulation can hinder your seeds from growing. Negative stimulation can distort messages, discourage progress, and even stop growth. Stopping negative stimulation can be done by cutting off the TV, turning off the radio, and going into a room where your space is distraction-free. Sometimes, this means closing your blinds or shades or waiting until everyone else in your house goes to sleep.

If others in your household go to sleep too late, you can also try waking up earlier than everybody else. Sometimes if you have the resources, going to another place altogether may help remove distractions. Sometimes, community libraries have nice places, and some university libraries have study rooms. In more extreme cases, there are options like getting a hotel room with a pool or a nice

The Growth Principle

bathtub or Jacuzzi to remove all distractions to foster growth.

Removing physical distractions, relaxing and meditating can help you remove mental distractions. Some people may have intense pressure on them to finish a task, or may be preoccupied with a recent failed relationship, but a clear mind is just as important to creating a sub-environment as a clear space.

The second step to creating a positive sub-environment is to add positive stimulation in your surroundings. It's not enough just to get rid of negative stimulation; it's also important to add positive stimulation. Positive stimulation consists of things that are encouraging, uplifting and foster growth toward your vision for your future. As we know, any seed planted and nurtured will grow only when it has the right environment. Your positive stimulation should be related to the seeds that you're beginning to plant. For instance, if you are trying to plant the seed of self-esteem, your positive stimulation should be fostering self-esteem. Your environment should be a place where you can feel respected and valued, because those factors are what will fertilize your seeds and foster growth.

Creating positive stimulation can be accomplished in a variety of ways. It can be created by playing soft music to calm your mind and remove stress and distractions. You can use motivational speaking or religious preaching to help create an environment conducive to growth. Or, you can also read or surround yourself with positive messages that move you to extraordinary accomplishment. The ideas presented may be intuitive or something you may have heard before, but the reality is that not many people put into practice the things that will facilitate their growth, and now is your opportunity.

Reflections

1. What distractions have prevented me from reaching my goals?

_____
_____
_____
_____
_____
_____
_____
_____

2. What things can I put in place to help create a positive environment?

_____
_____
_____
_____
_____
_____
_____
_____

Chapter 7: Nurture Your Seeds

Any seed that's planted but never watered will not grow. That's why it's important to make sure that every seed you plant is well nurtured and well supported. Seeds that are supported, cared for, and cultivated will produce a plentiful and effective harvest.

How to nurture your seeds

There are a few values that are essential to nurturing your seeds. These values can make the difference in a seed producing fruit effectively in one year or a seed producing fruit inefficiently in seven years. Just as grass seeds need water, your personal seeds need nurturing through values that will fertilize your growth.

Self-discipline

The first value that is vital to your seed's health is self-discipline. Every plentiful harvest is built on the foundational value of discipline. Discipline is important, because it ensures that effective strategies are favored and strived for over ineffective strategies. When many people hear the word discipline, they remember painful experiences of childhood mischief and associate the word with punishment. However, **discipline** is not punishment and will be defined as "self-controlled behavior determined by guidelines." In other words, having discipline is exemplifying behavior that is consistent with one's goals and objectives.

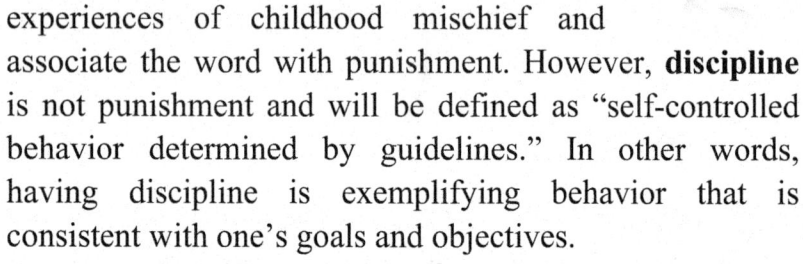

For instance, if your goal is to lose 50 pounds in 3 months, any behavior that isn't consistent with that goal would be a behavior outside of discipline. Another example is if your objective was to save $2,000 in 6 months, by not spending more than $100 on entertainment each month. But, if you always spent $300+ a month on entertainment items, your actions are not consistent with your goal, and therefore not disciplined.

It's one thing to have a great vision, and effective seeds, but without the discipline to plant and nurture those seeds, they will just fall on unfertile ground. I can remember having the vision to write a book about personal growth. I was motivated and excited about what I had to share with the world. I investigated what seeds I would need to plant to make it grow and created a sub-environment to make it happen.

However, on my first try, I failed to become committed to the discipline I needed to get it done. I would lose focus and begin exhibiting actions that were not consistent with the seeds I was trying to plant and the vision I developed. I soon had to realize that if I wanted to nurture the seeds I was planting, and see this book come to fruition, I would have to discipline myself and remove all behaviors that were not consistent with my goals. After I stayed disciplined, I was able to write the very book you are reading today.

Patience

The second value that is vital to your seed's health is patience. Just as many wise people have said "patience is a virtue," it is more of a virtue today than ever before. **Patience** is simply defined *as tolerating delayed preference without complaint.* Patience is something that will protect you against the harmful tapestry of anxiety, worry, apprehension and frustration. These negative qualities will make you poison the seed that you've already planted and restrict your vision from fully manifesting.

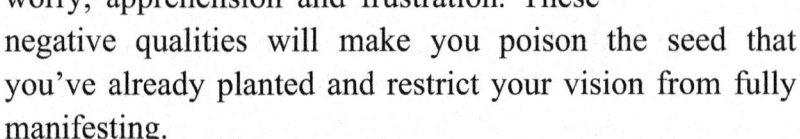

The Bible even teaches us the importance and value of having and expressing patience. In the Book of James chapter 1 verses 2 through 4, it says: "My brethren, count it all joy when ye fall into divers temptations; Knowing this, that the trying of your faith worketh patience. But let patience have her perfect work, that ye may be perfect and entire, wanting nothing."

The Bible helps us to understand that when temptations come to test our faith, we should resist getting discouraged or anxious and apprehensive. Instead, you should know that this is an opportunity to build your faith, and that no matter what happens, you already are fulfilled and happy with life.

Imagine if your patience builds a type of peace that would not have you going up and down like a ship lost at sea when things were tough, but would have you calm and fulfilled because you know you "want for nothing." I realize that if I had all the money in the world, but didn't have peace and patience, it wouldn't be worth it. I know that if I had all the fame in the world and couldn't be patient, I'd give every ounce of fame back in a second.

The value of patience can prevent you from poisoning the seed you worked hard to plant. Patience helps us understand it's okay that change doesn't happen in a day and that your vision may take a little extra time to reach completion. Those things are reasonable and can be expected. Even though your preference is delayed, your fulfillment is always delivered.

Focus

The third value that is essential to nurturing your seed is the value of focus. Just as a camera out of focus will not take a clear picture, a seed planted without focus will not have a clear harvest. Many seeds are planted when people are motivated, inspired and encouraged. However, after seven days of living life, and dealing with the vicissitudes of your social climate, it becomes very easy to lose focus and discontinue nurturing your seeds.

To battle against the issue of lack of focus, it is important to create what's called a focus board. A **focus board** is something that is seen by you every day. The purpose of the focus board is to remind you of your vision, and more important, *the seeds you are planting to reach that vision*. These aren't necessarily things that are tangible; often times they are intangible: your seeds.

Seeds accomplished or fully nurtured should be able to be easily removed, so new seeds can be displayed. The focus board is a way of proving to yourself (and others) that you are taking the growth process seriously. If you find that you are lacking in the desire to even complete a focus board, then you must ask yourself about your true desire to grow. If you can't seem to find where you should place your focus board, that's okay. Your focus board could be placed on your bathroom mirror, your closet door, or your bedroom window. Just remember that, as long as you see it every day, it can be effective. It's much less effective if you place it somewhere that only graces your presence every couple of days.

Remember that your focus board acts as a reminder of what you should be focusing on and what behaviors should be used throughout your day.

Adaptability

The fourth value that will help effectively nurture your seeds is the value of adaptability. Just as you strive to be ever changing, the world is also an ever-changing place. **Adaptability** simply means your ability to alter methods to be more effective and efficient. Adaptability is an important value for nurturing your seeds, because what might have worked yesterday may not work tomorrow. You must be aware of your effectiveness and efficiency throughout your growth. If you find your methods or strategies for planting and

The Growth Principle

growing seeds becomes inadequate at any time, you must be able to adapt.

Bill Gates, founder of the software giant Microsoft, said in 1981 that "640k ought to be enough for anybody." He was talking about a computer and saying that 640K (which is a little over a half a megabyte, or about 1/2000th of a Gigabyte) is enough memory for any personal use. You won't have to go far to learn that many computers of today use well over 640K for memory or hard drive space. Many computers today are using Terabytes (TB) to classify storage (1TB = 1 Trillion bytes), which is more than a million times more than the 640K of the 1980s. The point is that Bill Gates, and other people who want to stay effective, had to continually adapt; the same is true of people who want to reach extraordinary accomplishment.

The Growth Principle

Reflections

1. What are some things that should go on my focus board?

_____
_____
_____
_____
_____
_____
_____
_____
_____
_____

2. How could adaptability help me plant and nurture my personal seeds?

_____
_____
_____
_____
_____
_____
_____
_____
_____
_____

Chapter 8: Work Your Plan

"Genius is one percent inspiration and 99 percent perspiration."
- Thomas Edison

Many people make the mistake of thinking that change and growth happen in an instant. The reality is that change doesn't happen in an instant, although *a decision to change* can be made in an instant. Making a decision to change should not be confused with changing itself. Change and growth happen through a process of consistency, not just a moment of contentment. The reason change is a process is because it is defined by your future action, not just your present inspiration. It's good to have inspiration, but realize that change and growth are things that take consistent work, not just spontaneous desire. That's why it's important not only to plan your work, but also to work your plan.

G.J. Barnes

Work Your Plan Now

"The path of least resistance will leave a man and a river crooked."
- Native American Proverb

As I stated before, change is based on future action. However, we must understand that in order to make change in the future, we must start the process of growth now in the present. As we begin our process for consistent change, we must make sure that our process *begins*. Even if you don't see it, every second your body is growing. We tend to notice change overtime at the end result, but the reality is that a little change happens every day.

Even though our ambition is to move forward and look for our growth in the future, it is important that we act upon our objective now, and not later. The key to remember is to start working your plan NOW! Don't wait for circumstances to look better, because either you have to make them look better yourself, or they will never get better. You can start your growth from any place under the sun. The important thing is that you do start, and you keeping pressing forward.

The Growth Principle

I can remember counseling several people about growth and change, and many people would agree that growth and change was needed. However, they would always object to beginning, because they would consistently say, "I'm not ready yet." I would always try to respond in a loving and caring manner with, "The fact that you're not ready, means you're ready." The point that we think we're not ready, says to me, we're in need of growth, and if we're in need of growth, that means we're ready for growth.

As you move to create an attitude of acting now, it is helpful to analyze and measure your growth along the way. An example of this type of measurement may be setting aside time every week to reflect on what you've done to reach your vision by journaling. You also may consider a weekly or bi-weekly discussion with close friends or family members about your experiences and challenges. This type of interaction helps facilitate your do-it-now approach and subsequently increases your productivity. As we discussed before, consistency is the key, so make sure that your assessment is done regularly. I would suggest that your evaluation doesn't have to be formal, but it does have to be consistent.

Reflections

1. Have I had any good ideas that I never followed through on?

___

2. Have I ever given up on something because it wasn't perfect?

___

Chapter 9: Things That Hinder Your Work

1. Not Knowing Where to Start

Not knowing where to start is one of the easiest things to fix. That's because when you don't know where to start, you start exactly where you are. Hopefully, the process of investigating your seeds would have given you the first seed to plant. Once you have that, plant that seed, and begin the change process from right where you are. Some people may be closer to their seed's fruit than others, but that's perfectly okay.

There are some that may feel that they are so far from even seeing their first fruit, they shouldn't even begin the process. But, the truth is you can't afford not to begin the process. If your first seed seems like it's too much of a challenge, it might be appropriate to add another step (another seed) to help you get to the next point. Adding another step to the seed planting process just means that you add another seed that is more appropriate for you to reach your goal.

For example, if your first seed is to spend more time with your family, and there just seems to be 50 things stopping you from seeing that fruit, then you might want to plant a seed before that, such as starting a time evaluation log. A **time evaluation log** is simply a log that records where you spend your time, so that you are better able to evaluate how you spend your day. This extra seed can help you get to the next seed of spending more time with your family.

2. Laziness

Being lazy is something that can have a long list of possible causes, but the bottom line is it results in nothing. Laziness basically means that you don't want to start any form of work, because work is essentially work. More deeply, laziness means that you have gotten too comfortable in your idleness.

Despite the many psychological causes of laziness, there are some simple ways to eliminate it. To combat chronic laziness, first consider the cause. Does your laziness come from deep psychological problems, such as really being afraid of rejection (see chapter 3) or is it something like not having enough physical energy? For

The Growth Principle

something like not having a lot of physical energy, we must begin to look at maximizing our bodies' physical effectiveness.

The most frequent cause of this type of physical lethargy is not getting *enough* sleep. Sure people do go to sleep, but there is an overwhelming number of people who don't get *enough* sleep. A small group of people don't get sufficient sleep because of biological problems that may need a medical course of treatment. But, the vast majority of people simply don't get enough sleep because they stay up too late and have to wake up very early.

Basically, many of us need to adopt a serious regimen of steady sleeping habits. The average adult needs to get somewhere close to eight full hours of sleep, but many get only five or six. If those numbers are representative of an average person's rest, then people usually miss about 32 percent of their needed sleep every night. Imagine that you could be missing around 32 percent of your potential every day. If you were to combine that figure over the long run, you could be enormously inadequate in your mental and physical capacity simply due to a lack of rest.

Another thing to consider in our discovery of the causes of laziness is diet. The body is built so that it must have the proper nutrients and food to work at its highest level of efficiency and effectiveness. If one were to put alcohol into a car, would you expect it to run at its best? Surely not, especially since the car was designed to run off of unleaded gasoline. The same is true of our precious bodies. Our bodies weren't designed to run off of junk food, soda, and grease. Rather, our bodies were built and designed by God to run off of needed vitamins, minerals and natural foods to perform at their highest levels of efficiency and effectiveness.

According to the current United States Department of Agriculture, people should get a variety of food every day. The chart below is just an example of what a 40 year old healthy male and female would need on a daily basis.

(Age) Gender	Whole Grains	Vegetables	Fruits	Milk	Meat & Beans	Moderate Physical Activity
(40) Female	3 ounces	2.5 cups	1.5 cups	3 cups	5 ounces	15-20 minutes
(40) Male	4 ounces	3 cups	2 cups	3 cups	6.5 ounces	15-20 minutes

After we've considered our rest and diet, we must take into account our environment. I can remember in my college days when I moved off of campus, and was living at home with my parents. There were several times when I tried to study for a big test, but I just couldn't seem to study in my bedroom. As a result, I can remember picking up a book that helped people learn how to study. One of the first things it said was to study in the proper environment. I remember the author talking about people associating places with feelings, and feeling with actions. Because of that, it was suggested to never study in your bedroom, since your bedroom is associated with sleep and leisure. This made sense to me, and when I moved my studying to the library, I noticed a big improvement in my grades.

  The point I'm making is that for some things to change and to get done, your have to change your environment. Some of our living rooms are associated with laziness (and that's okay), but if we are trying to implement change (especially something involving a physical change) in that environment and finding it difficult, it may be time for a change of scenery. It may be a good idea for you to join a gym, or read at your local library. The reality is that laziness can be fostered by your environment.

3. Procrastination

  Another thing that can stop your work flow is the ever-lurking presence of the enemy called procrastination. Procrastination is something that I'm sure many of us have danced with at one time or another in life. We've seen the temptation of this monster creep up into our everyday activities, and it loves to tell us: "You can do it later." However, we must be strong and willing to tell this monkey to flee from our back for once and for all. Procrastination is mostly a promise that never delivers. You think that you'll have time to complete your deed later; however, time always runs out, and you always wish you had done it earlier.

Procrastination can have a long list of potential causes. However, the bottom line is that procrastination must be met with a "do it now" attitude. There are many books that will go much deeper into the causes and treatments of chronic procrastination, but the bottom line is that procrastination must be stopped, and the only way to do that is to do what you have to do when you have to do it. When you are working your plan, planting your seeds, and writing down your vision, hold yourself responsible (and have your accountability partner hold you responsible as well) for getting things done on time. Even if it doesn't work the first time, make sure you never give up on your growth, and keep holding yourself responsible for getting things done on time.

"If what you are doing is worth doing, then hang in there until it is done."
-Nido Qubein

The Growth Principle

I can remember being at a psychological conference and hearing a research Professor present a study about how learning occurs. The conclusion was that the pathways and procedures of learning in the brain cannot be undone; they can only be redone. In other words, you can't unlearn something, but you can relearn something.

The reality is that you will not be able to unlearn bad habits that are detrimental to your growth, but you will be able to learn new habits that will supersede the old ones. It is important that you know that relearning is important. It must be done with conviction and dedication. When you are working your plan, know that relearning takes practice. It is okay if all your goals don't seem to be going as easily as planned. Just know that the most important thing in the process of relearning is to keep trying.

I believe that never giving up is the single thing most strongly correlated with growth. Sure it is mentioned in the beginning, middle and ending of this book, but that is simply because every other truth falls under that principle.

Reflections

1. How has procrastination stopped me from reaching my goals in the past?

___

2. Do I get enough sleep at night to be fully productive throughout the day?

___

The Growth Principle

Chapter 10: Have Faith in Your Success

Faith makes us sure of what we hope for and gives us proof of what we cannot see.
(Hebrews 11:1 CEV)

I can remember being so excited about the new piece of furniture that my family and I were purchasing. I saw a display of the wood and glass shelf we'd buy and couldn't wait to get it in our family room. I casually summoned the clerk to get a brand new shelf for purchase from the back, and after I swiped my credit card, we carried the 100 pound wood and glass shelf to my SUV. When I got home, I plunged into prying the box open and spilling out the 20 or so pieces to put this shelf together.

I can recall it was at that very moment that my excitement level dropped like a baseball falling from a homerun hit. The reason for this sudden change came from the 30+ pieces scattered across my family room floor. I couldn't believe that the beautifully built wood and glass shelf had a beginning that looked like this. There were so many pieces, tools, and screws that I couldn't fathom this pile of wood and glass being transformed into the beautiful shelf that I saw on the cover of the box, let alone me having the ability to make such a transition.

As I sat down and realized that I wasn't going to take the product back to the store, I picked up the 40+ page instruction manual (it was written in 4 different languages) and began to search for the pieces in step one. Piece after piece, I began to fasten one thing to another. One screw here, one door here, and another base there. After about five steps, I could vaguely start to see how this shelf would be put together. It was interesting because the first couple of steps didn't seem like they were working toward the final product. But, to my surprise, those steps were vital to the success and accomplishment of building this wonderful piece of furniture.

The lesson and experience from building this shelve applies to growth. There may be times when your journey, self-discipline and hard work seem like they have nothing to do with accomplishing your objective of growth, but if we keep the faith and stay dedicated to the plan, you will surely get to the great place of you "Promised Land" and extraordinary accomplishment. It simply requires you to

The Growth Principle

have faith in success, even if you don't always see the evidence up front.

Truth vs. fact

Having faith in our success as we implement our seed planting is based on a foundational way of thinking. That way of thinking is defined by being focused on truth and not just the facts. To put it in basic terms, facts only categorize *what is happening based on evidence*, but the truth speaks of *what will happen based on faith*. For example, the fact may be that you are trying to quit smoking, and you are currently smoking one pack a day.

Yes, that is a fact. That's based on the current evidence that we see in front of us. However, through faith, the truth is that you can stop smoking if you believe you can and, if you follow up with your effort, faith and determination, you will stop smoking. The point is which way of thinking do you implement and focus on? Going back to a sentence in the beginning of the book, will we be focused on the problem, or will we be focused on the pledge? We could focus on where we are (or where we're not), or *we can focus on where we will be and stay.*

Faith Creates Results

Over the years, I've been blessed to learn that having faith in your success and accomplishment doesn't just give you hope; it gives you results. Having a faith mindset will put you in positions that will elevate your circumstances. For instance, having faith and belief in getting that good job you have your eye on will cause you to revise your resume, write a cover letter, and submit your materials to the human resource officer.

Imagine that you didn't have a faith mindset and didn't believe in the possibility of your getting that job. Would you have taken the time to tweak your resume, or write a cover letter, or submit your materials? I'm sure you can see how having faith doesn't just give you hope; it gives you opportunities to create your success. The bottom line is that faith creates action, and action creates results.

Reflections

1. How many doubts do I have regarding my ability to accomplish extraordinary things?

_____
_____
_____
_____
_____
_____
_____
_____
_____

2. In the past, how have facts deterred me from realizing the truth?

_____
_____
_____
_____
_____
_____
_____
_____
_____
_____

Chapter 11: Strengthen Others

"Charity begins at home and justice begins next door."
- Charles Dickens

It is important to understand that when one reaches growth, it is imperative to help others grow. Just as trees that are mature drop more seeds into the ground, we should spread and plant seeds into other people. Why? Because, one tree can provide enough fruit to feed a family, but a forest can provide enough fruit to feed a nation. As we remember from earlier chapters, the fruit we manifest isn't just for us, but for others as well. So, as we grow together, we can all reap the blessings of our collective fruit and all reach extraordinary accomplishment.

G.J. Barnes

We must be actively thinking about how we are strengthening others. It must be something that is a part of our daily thoughts and concerns. Just as we are striving for growth in ourselves, we must also be striving for growth in others.

Why we don't strengthen others

In western society, capitalism has done great things for our economy and great things for our wealth. With capitalism, we have grown multinational corporations and family-owned local businesses. We've created millions of jobs and generated enough capital to donate billions of dollars to people and organizations in need. However, one of the main tenets and characteristics of capitalism is the creation of "winners," at the expense of "losers." With capitalism, we've taken what was successful in our economic development and allowed that to seep into the tapestry of our moral development.

Many times we seem to be happy or successful only if we win, and by definition, that means someone else loses. Just think of sports. Millions of Westerners (and

The Growth Principle

cultures that may resemble Western behavior) cherish sports. We love to see our favorite teams win, and we love to see our not-so-favorite teams lose. But, what seed does this plant into our minds? Well, the subconscious message is that winning is a singular event. In order for one to win, others must lose. If we think about it, in sports and other competitive areas, winners are classified as those who "do better" than "losers." It's very interesting because, if you were to ask any kid in the third grade what's the opposite of winners, I'm sure that she would easily and confidently say, "Losers."

If winning is the opposite of losing, then how do we regard all of those hard-working athletes and other professionals that don't win? At the end of the day, we simply classify them as losers.

Here is my suggestion, if we are to engage in competitive actions, the best performer should not be classified as a winner, but as a leading figure, or a leading team, or a leading athlete. The term leading does not degrade all the people and teams that didn't make that position and it leaves room to foster self-esteem. We must take after the fire that rests on a candle and know that when its light is shared, it loses nothing, but accomplishes everything.

It is important to know that, as we embrace our accomplishment, we embrace others' accomplishments. As we strive for our achievement, we must strive for others' achievements. And, we must remember to keep the words of John Wesley close to our hearts: "Do all the good you can, by all the means you can, in all the ways you can, in all the places you can, at all the times you can, to all the people you can, as long as ever you can."

Reflections

1. How many people have I personally helped to accomplish something?

_____
_____
_____
_____
_____
_____
_____
_____

2. How many people will benefit from the seeds I sow in the present and future?

_____
_____
_____
_____
_____
_____

Appendix

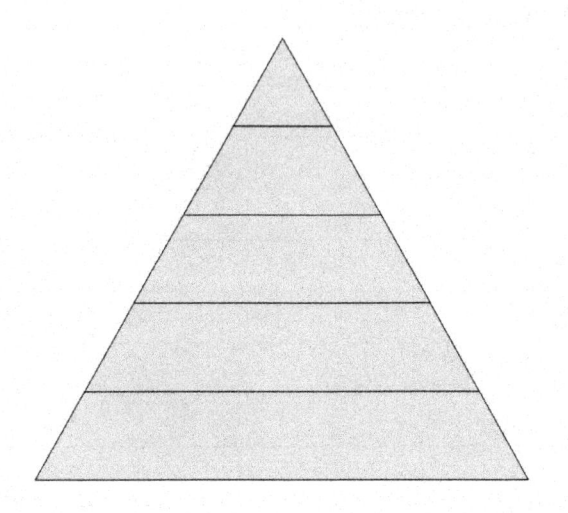

The Growth Principle

Barnes Family Foundational Statement
September 20th 2005

1. To intensify our appreciation of God's love, word, and power.

2. To exemplify love, joy, peace, longsuffering, kindness, goodness, faithfulness, meekness and self-control.

3. To emulate God's Infinite Wisdom.

4. To be intentional and expeditious in needed change and growth.

5. To be unconditionally committed to loving (1 Corinthians 13:4-8) and prioritizing our spouse.

6. To be unified as a family in loving each other, embodying and following Christ.

7. To seek, acquire, and apply knowledge effectively.

8. To learn and apply habits that promotes health, and optimal physical condition.

9. To acquire financial freedom that establishes an inheritance for future generations.

10. To be efficient and effective leaders in family, social, and spiritual development.

11. To have a successful, efficient and progressive business.

12. To be dedicated to empowering, encouraging, and providing resources to those in need.

CPSIA information can be obtained at www.ICGtesting.com
Printed in the USA
BVOW05s2245110916

461825BV00001B/3/P

9 781432 726447